Prompt Engineering Secrets

T.S. AVINI

Prompt Engineering Secrets

The Art and Science of Talking to AI Like a Pro

by T.S. AVINI

Reader Note

This book is for educational and informational purposes. Use the ideas as general guidance and adapt them to your personal situation.

Using this guide: keep a notebook nearby, mark useful ideas, and turn the examples into simple actions you can repeat during the week.

Table of Contents

Chapter 1: Introduction: The Emergence of Prompt Engineering

The dawn of the 21st century has been marked by unprecedented advances in technology, with artificial intelligence (AI) standing at the forefront of these innovations.

As AI systems have evolved from rudimentary data processing machines to sophisticated entities capable of complex decision-making, the ways in which humans interact with these systems have also transformed. At the very heart of this transformation lies prompt engineering, an emerging discipline that is rapidly redefining how we communicate with intelligent machines.

Prompt engineering first garnered attention with the advent of large language models such as OpenAI's GPT-3 and its successors. These models, capable of generating coherent, contextually relevant text in response to input prompts, represented a significant leap forward in natural language processing (NLP).

However, the effectiveness of these models is contingent upon the quality of interaction initiated by the user—specifically, the prompts provided to the system. It was quickly recognized that the manner in which questions and commands are framed can dramatically influence the outcome of an AI's response. Thus, prompt engineering emerged not just as a technique, but as an art form, blending linguistic intuition with technical acumen.

At first glance, A critical factor driving the need for prompt engineering is the inherent complexity and variability of human language. Natural language does not adhere to strict rules; it is fluid, context-dependent, and often ambiguous.

This poses significant challenges for AI systems trained to understand and generate human-like text. Prompt engineering seeks to bridge this gap by crafting input queries that are clear, specific, and aligned with the model's capabilities. Through deliberate experimentation and refinement, practitioners of prompt engineering aim to coax optimal performance from AI systems, tailoring the interaction to meet specific objectives.

At its core, prompt engineering draws from principles of linguistics, cognitive science, and computer science. Linguistically, it necessitates an understanding of syntax, semantics, and pragmatics to construct prompts that are precise and unambiguous.

From a cognitive standpoint, it requires an awareness of how humans naturally process language and concepts, as well as how AI models interpret and simulate these processes. Technically, prompt engineering must account for the unique architecture and training data of each AI system, leveraging their strengths and compensating for their limitations.

One of the most intriguing aspects of prompt engineering is its potential for creative exploration. Unlike traditional programming, which is often deterministic and rule-based, prompt engineering allows for exploratory iteration.

Users can experiment with different phrasing, styles, and constructs to elicit varied responses from the AI, fostering a dynamic and interactive dialogue. This creative aspect not only enhances the utility and versatility of AI models but also democratizes access to advanced AI capabilities—no longer is extensive programming knowledge a prerequisite to harnessing the power of AI.

Moreover, prompt engineering has wide-ranging applications across numerous fields. In content creation, it enables writers and marketers to generate engaging and relevant material efficiently.

In education, it supports personalized learning experiences by adapting the level and style of instruction to the needs of individual students. In customer service, it empowers chatbots to handle complex queries with nuanced understanding and empathy. The versatility of prompt engineering underscores its importance as a fundamental skill in the digital age.

The rise of prompt engineering also raises important ethical considerations. As AI systems become increasingly adept at simulating human-like conversation, it is imperative to ensure that these interactions are transparent and accountable.

There is a risk that poorly constructed prompts could lead to biased or misleading outcomes, particularly if the AI's training data contains implicit biases. As such, prompt engineers bear the responsibility of not only refining the technical aspects of their craft but also upholding ethical standards in AI interactions.

To understand the nuances of prompt engineering, one must appreciate the iterative nature of the process. It often involves crafting numerous variations of a prompt, analyzing the outputs, and making incremental adjustments to achieve the desired response.

This iterative cycle is akin to a dialogue between the user and the AI—an ongoing conversation that refines understanding and builds towards precision. Prompt engineering is not merely about asking questions; it is about asking the right questions in the right way.

Believe it or not, In conclusion, the emergence of prompt engineering represents a pivotal development in the field of artificial intelligence. It encapsulates the convergence of language, technology, and creativity, offering a new paradigm for interacting with intelligent systems.

As AI continues to evolve, the importance of effective communication between humans and machines will only grow, underscoring the relevance of prompt engineering as both a skill and an art form. In this rapidly advancing technological landscape, those who master the intricacies of prompt engineering will possess a key to unlocking the full potential of AI, transforming it from a tool of utility into a partner in innovation.

Chapter 2: Understanding Artificial Intelligence: A Primer

Artificial Intelligence (AI) has emerged as one of the most transformative technologies of the modern era.

To harness its potential, it's essential to understand its core principles, methodologies, and applications. This chapter serves as a comprehensive primer on AI, providing insights into its foundations, evolution, and contemporary landscape.

What is Artificial Intelligence?

To be honest, Artificial Intelligence can be defined as the field of computer science that focuses on creating machines capable of performing tasks that normally require human intelligence.

These tasks encompass a wide array of functions, including visual perception, speech recognition, decision-making, language translation, and even complex problem-solving. AI systems are designed to replicate cognitive functions such as learning and problem-solving, which are associated with human intellect.

One of the key characteristics of AI is its ability to learn from data.

This involves the process where computers are programmed to receive input data, process it, and improve their performance over time without explicit human instructions. This learning capability is central to the development of robust AI systems.

The Evolution of AI

In real life, Understanding AI requires a glimpse into its history.

The term "artificial intelligence" was first coined in 1956 by John McCarthy during a summer conference at Dartmouth College. The early years of AI were marked by optimism, with researchers making significant strides in programming computers to solve algebra problems and play games like chess.

The 1970s and 1980s, however, saw the onset of what is known as the "AI winter" — a period of reduced funding and interest due to unfulfilled promises and limitations in computational power.

It wasn't until the mid-1990s that AI entered a renaissance, driven by advancements in machine learning and the availability of substantial computational resources.

Today, AI encompasses a broad range of technologies, with machine learning, deep learning, natural language processing, and robotics as prominent subfields.

The exponential growth of data and advancements in algorithms have propelled AI to the forefront of technological innovation.

Core Concepts in AI

Machine Learning

At the heart of AI lies machine learning (ML), a method that enables computers to learn from data.

Unlike traditional software that follows pre-programmed rules, ML algorithms identify patterns and relationships within datasets and use them to make predictions or decisions. Key types of machine learning include supervised learning, unsupervised learning, and reinforcement learning.

- **Supervised Learning**: In supervised learning, algorithms are trained on labeled data.

The model learns to map input data to the correct output. Common applications include image classification and speech recognition.

- **Unsupervised Learning**: This approach deals with unlabeled data, aiming to identify hidden structures or patterns without explicit guidance on what to learn.

Clustering and association are typical techniques used in unsupervised learning.

- **Reinforcement Learning**: In reinforcement learning, an agent learns to make decisions by receiving feedback in the form of rewards or penalties.

This method is particularly useful in environments where an AI must learn to interact with and modify its surroundings, such as in gaming or autonomous driving.

Neural Networks and Deep Learning

Neural networks, inspired by the human brain's architecture, are pivotal in deep learning, a subset of ML that involves layers of computational nodes to process data.

These networks enable AI to perform tasks that involve sequential data synthesis, like language translation and image recognition.

Deep learning models are efficient at handling large volumes of unstructured data and have powered breakthroughs in achieving near-human-level performance in complex tasks, including medical diagnosis and automated navigation.

Natural Language Processing

A subfield of AI, natural language processing (NLP), focuses on the interaction between computers and humans through language.

NLP aims to enable computers to interpret, generate, and respond to human language in a meaningful way.

NLP encompasses several tasks such as sentiment analysis, machine translation, and conversational agents (chatbots).

The progress in NLP is driven by advanced algorithms capable of understanding context, sentiment, and even humor, creating more intuitive human-computer dialogues.

Applications of AI

AI's applications span numerous domains, and its influence is pervasive. In healthcare, AI is utilized for diagnostic assistance, treatment personalization, and patient monitoring.

In finance, AI-driven systems are deployed for fraud detection, risk assessment, and customer service automation. Additionally, AI is revolutionizing sectors like transportation, where it is integral to developing autonomous vehicles, and retail, by enhancing supply chain management and customer personalization.

AI's potential extends to scientific research, arts, and education.

Innovative AI models are used in drug discovery, content creation, and personalized learning environments, aiming to tackle global challenges and foster creativity.

Ethical and Societal Implications

As AI continues to evolve, it poses significant ethical and societal challenges.

These include concerns over privacy, bias in AI models, and the impact of AI on employment. Ensuring transparency, accountability, and fairness in AI systems is critical to fostering public trust.

Research communities and industries are actively developing guidelines and regulatory frameworks to address these concerns.

Encouraging ethical AI innovation, robust data governance, and inclusive policy-making are pivotal steps towards equitable AI deployment.

Final Thoughts

Artificial Intelligence, a field once confined to science fiction, has become an indispensable part of contemporary society.

Understanding the fundamental concepts of AI, from its learning algorithms to its wide-ranging applications, empowers individuals across disciplines to interact effectively with these technologies.

In this ever-evolving landscape, staying informed about AI's capabilities and limitations is crucial.

By grasping the intricacies of how AI works, individuals can leverage its power responsibly and creatively, shaping a future where humans and machines coexist harmoniously. As we continue to unlock AI's potential, a firm grounding in its principles will be instrumental for anyone aspiring to master the art and science of engaging with artificial intelligence.

Chapter 3: The Evolution of Human-Machine Communication

In the rapidly expanding field of artificial intelligence, the way we interact with machines has evolved remarkably over the decades.

This evolution reflects not only technological advancements but also changes in how we perceive and utilize these technologies. The communication between humans and machines has transformed from rudimentary input commands to sophisticated, nuanced dialogues facilitated by advanced language models.

Early Beginnings: Command and Control

Interestingly enough, The journey of human-machine communication began in the mid-20th century, with the advent of early computers. These machines were controlled through binary systems and punch cards, requiring meticulous and precise inputs that left little room for error.

The user-machine interface was limited to command-line inputs, a stark contrast to the intuitive interfaces we interact with today. Communication with machines at this stage was heavily dependent on syntax; even a slight deviation could result in system errors or command failures.

During this era, the human factor was a critical constraint.

Users were required to possess specialized knowledge of programming languages to interact with computers. This mode of communication was unidirectional — users 'told' machines what to do, and machines executed the tasks without an understanding or inferencing capability.

The Graphical User Interface Revolution

Let's not forget, The introduction of graphical user interfaces (GUIs) in the 1980s marked a significant turning point in human-machine communication. By incorporating visual elements like windows, icons, and menus, GUIs democratized access to computers.

Users no longer needed to memorize complex command lines; instead, they could interact with machines through direct manipulation of objects on the screen. This transition from text-based to image-based interaction paved the way for broader adoption of computers across various industries and the general public.

GUIs served as the first step towards a more intuitive and natural interaction with machines.

They changed how tasks were conceptualized and executed, focusing on user experience over rigid command formats. The human-machine interaction became bidirectional to some extent, with systems responding to user actions through visual feedback.

Natural Language Processing: Bridging the Gap

Many people don't realize this, but As computer systems grew more sophisticated, the need for a more natural form of communication became apparent.

Natural Language Processing (NLP), a subfield of AI and linguistics, emerged as the essential bridge to achieve this goal. NLP aims to facilitate interaction between humans and machines using natural language as opposed to structured commands.

In the late 20th century, developments in NLP started to gain momentum, though early systems were rudimentary, often failing to understand context or ambiguity.

However, these systems laid the groundwork for future advancements by emphasizing the importance of semantics and syntax in language.

The progression of NLP technology paralleled improvements in computational power and data availability.

Techniques such as parsing, sentiment analysis, and information retrieval became increasingly sophisticated, allowing more nuanced understanding and generation of human language by machines. This evolution enabled the development of applications like chatbots, virtual assistants, and language translation services, which became more reliable and user-friendly over time.

The AI Revolution: Conversational Agents and Machine Learning

With the dawn of the 21st century, AI technology experienced a revolution driven by advancements in machine learning, particularly deep learning.

Conversational agents, such as Siri, Alexa, and Google's Assistant, emerged as a new frontier in human-machine communication. These agents were designed to understand, learn, and process natural language, enabling more dynamic and responsive interaction.

Machine learning techniques, particularly neural networks, contributed significantly to this evolution.

By processing and learning from vast datasets, these systems became capable of recognizing patterns, understanding context, and even predicting user intent. Deep learning models, especially those focused on language, became adept at tasks like speech recognition, language translation, and conversational simulation.

I've seen this happen before: Recent advances in transformers and large language models, notably OpenAI's GPT series, have further propelled this field.

These models are capable of generating human-like text, engaging in coherent dialogues, and performing language tasks with unprecedented accuracy. They introduced a new dimension to human-machine communication, where machines can not only understand and respond but also generate creative content and solutions.

The Present: Dialogue Systems and Beyond

Today, we find ourselves at a fascinating crossroads where AI, powered by complex language models, can engage in meaningful dialogues with humans.

The technology has evolved from executing commands to participating in interactive communications that resemble human-to-human interactions. Dialogue systems are now capable of maintaining context over extended conversations, adapting responses, and even exhibiting personality traits as designed by developers.

To be honest, These systems are continuously improving their ability to handle a range of communication nuances, including emotional cues, idiomatic expressions, and cultural references.

As they become more sophisticated, they also raise ethical considerations regarding bias, transparency, and dependence on AI.

Future Trajectories: Towards Symbiotic Interaction

Looking ahead, the trajectory of human-machine communication is poised to become even more integrative and symbiotic.

The future may see the emergence of context-aware systems that intuitively understand user intentions across various domains, languages, and contexts. These systems will likely employ multimodal inputs, incorporating visual, auditory, and even emotional data to provide deeply personalized and meaningful interactions.

In real life, Moreover, advances in brain-computer interface technologies may reduce communication barriers even further, allowing for direct neural input into computers.

This could revolutionize the way we collaborate with machines, effectively blurring the lines between human thought and machine processing.

These developments highlight a significant shift towards a partnership model, where humans and machines collaboratively engage in problem-solving and creative processes.

As AI continues to evolve, the need for effective prompt engineering and the techniques to harness these interactions will remain crucial.

Chapter Takeaway

I've seen this happen before: The evolution of human-machine communication illustrates the profound impact of technological advancements on interaction methodologies.

From command-line interfaces to sophisticated dialogue systems, the journey underscores the importance of designing systems that are intuitive, responsive, and adaptive to human needs. As we move forward, prompt engineering will play a pivotal role in shaping this evolution, ensuring that communication remains seamless, effective, and beneficial to both humans and machines.

Chapter 4: The Science Behind AI Language Models

The fascinating world of artificial intelligence has seen exponential growth in recent years, with advancements in AI language models standing at the forefront of this technological evolution.

As we aim to become proficient in prompt engineering, it is imperative to grasp the intricate science underpinning these AI models. In this chapter, we delve into the mechanics, underlying theories, and critical advancements that have shaped modern AI language models such as GPT-3 and beyond.

At the core of AI language models lies the concept of machine learning, a subset of artificial intelligence that focuses on enabling machines to learn from data rather than being explicitly programmed. The specific branch of machine learning most pertinent to language models is deep learning, which utilizes neural networks with multiple layers to model complex patterns in data.

The architecture most commonly employed in language models today is the Transformer, introduced by Vaswani et al. in their landmark 2017 paper "Attention Is All You Need. ".

Transformers revolutionized the field by addressing the limitations of previous sequential models like Recurrent Neural Networks (RNNs) and Long Short-Term Memory (LSTM) networks. These earlier models struggled with processing long sequences due to issues like vanishing gradients, which hinder their ability to capture dependencies across distant words.

Transformers, however, eschew sequential processing in favor of a mechanism known as self-attention. This mechanism allows models to weigh the importance of different words in a sentence, thereby capturing contextual relationships more effectively.

The self-attention mechanism is a pivotal component of the Transformer architecture. It operates by creating attention scores that quantify the relevance of each word in a sentence concerning others.

Through a process known as scaled dot-product attention, these scores are calculated by taking the dot product of queries and keys, each derived from input embeddings, and scaling them by the square root of their dimension. This approach allows models to dynamically adjust their focus on various parts of a sentence, enabling them to discern nuances and complex syntactical structures.

Beyond self-attention, Transformers employ position encodings to retain the order of words, as their architecture inherently lacks this sequential information.

These encodings are added to input embeddings and are often derived using sine and cosine functions of varying frequencies, allowing the model to distinguish word positions effectively.

To be honest, Training large-scale language models involves extensive datasets and computational resources.

Models like OpenAI's GPT-3 are trained on hundreds of gigabytes of text data sourced from books, websites, and other repositories of human language. This diversity ensures a comprehensive understanding of varied linguistic structures and contexts but also requires sophisticated preprocessing to filter and clean the data to prevent the reinforcement of biases present in the training corpus.

Key to the training process is the optimization objective.

Language models typically leverage a technique called unsupervised learning, where they predict the likelihood of a word or sequence of words in a sentence. For Transformers, this often involves a pre-training phase where a model learns to fill in missing words (masked language modeling) and a fine-tuning phase where it is further adapted to specific tasks.

During the pre-training phase, the model learns a general representation of language, ingesting context from the large datasets mentioned previously.

It becomes adept at tasks like sentiment analysis, translation, and summarization by adjusting to new data during fine-tuning. This bifurcated process allows the model to achieve robustness and versatility, essential characteristics for responding to diverse user prompts.

Nevertheless, the significant advances in AI language models are not without challenges.

One major issue is the introduction and perpetuation of biases, as models trained on large datasets may inadvertently learn and replicate prejudices embedded within the data. Developers have introduced techniques like de-biasing and filtering to mitigate these effects, yet it remains an area of active research and ethical concern.

Moreover, while AI language models can generate impressively coherent and contextually appropriate outputs, their lack of genuine understanding poses limits.

These systems do not possess consciousness or comprehension akin to a human's; they perform statistical predictions based on input patterns. Addressing these limitations is critical for the development of models that can provide not only accurate but also genuinely meaningful and responsible interactions.

Several innovations are underway to enhance model capabilities, including few-shot and zero-shot learning, which allow models to perform tasks with minimal examples.

Reinforcement learning techniques like Reinforcement Learning from Human Feedback (RLHF) have also been integrated to align AI behaviors with human values.

Believe it or not, As we navigate the landscape of AI prompt engineering, appreciating the science behind language models equips us with the understanding needed to craft precise and effective interactions.

The complexity of these systems, rooted in deep learning and computational ingenuity, demands a careful balance between leveraging their capabilities and addressing their intrinsic limitations.

In the chapters that follow, we will explore techniques to harness the power of AI language models in practical applications.

By doing so, we aim to bridge the gap between theoretical comprehension and real-world utility, enabling readers to converse with AI in a manner that is both scientifically grounded and practically informed.

Chapter 5: Core Principles of Effective Prompt Engineering

Prompt engineering stands as a critical bridge between human cognitive demands and artificial intelligence capabilities.

In essence, crafting effective prompts is the art and science of communicating with AI systems in a way that ensures precision, relevance, and efficiency. This chapter explores the core principles essential for mastering prompt engineering, providing a solid foundation for users aiming to harness AI technologies effectively.

Understand the AI System

As strange as it sounds, To engineer successful prompts, one must first understand the AI system in use. This requires familiarity with the underlying model architecture, the type of data it was trained on, and any limitations it may possess.

For instance, most current natural language processing (NLP) models, such as those based on transformer architectures, excel at tasks involving pattern recognition in text. However, they may not cope well with purely abstract logic or tasks requiring real-time reasoning unavailable in their training data. Understanding these characteristics enables users to tailor prompts that align the system's strengths to the task at hand.

Clarity and Precision

A foundational principle is clarity. Prompts must be clear and explicit to elicit specific and accurate responses from AI systems. Ambiguities in prompting can lead to highly variable outputs, as AI models may interpret vague instructions in multiple valid ways.

Employing precise language, well-defined tasks, and disambiguated context ensures the AI interprets the prompt as intended. For instance, asking "Explain climate change in two sentences" provides more explicit guidance than "Tell me about climate change. ".

Contextual Framing

Effective prompt engineering leverages the power of context. This involves embedding sufficient background information within the prompt to guide the AI.

Integrating context can range from simple declarative statements that set the scene to complex multi-turn dialogues that build an informative narrative. When crafting context, one should avoid overwhelming details that could distract the AI. The goal is to balance necessary context with concise instruction to sustain focus on the primary task.

Iterative Refinement

Many people don't realize this, but Prompt engineering is a dynamic process demanding iterative refinement. Effective prompts seldom emerge fully-formed; they are the result of conscientious adaptation and experimentation.

Users should be prepared to test, evaluate, and repeatedly adjust their prompts. This iterative process allows the detection of unforeseen ambiguities, the enhancement of clarity, and the discovery of more effective phrasings. Iterative refinement is akin to an experimental loop, where feedback leads to more informed trials and increasingly reliable outputs.

Specify the Desired Output Format

Specifying the format or structure of the desired output can significantly reduce response variability and improve utility. This involves determining whether a response should be formatted as a list, a paragraph, a table, or even within a specific style such as formal or casual.

By clearly stating the expected format in the prompt, users guide the AI in producing outputs that match their requirements more precisely. For example, specifying "List the top five benefits of renewable energy" helps confine the AI's output within the requested format parameters.

Leveraging Exemplars

Providing exemplars is a powerful prompting technique that involves showing examples of the desired output within the prompt itself. This method can enhance the AI's understanding by illustrating the user's intentions explicitly.

Exemplars serve as live demonstrations of the expected style, substance, and format, allowing for an intuitive alignment of AI-generated responses with user expectations. Exemplars should be relevant, appropriately detailed, and consistent with the task objectives.

Consider Audience and Purpose

Effective prompt engineering also involves considering the ultimate audience and purpose of the AI output. This consideration influences the tone, complexity, and depth of information.

For example, prompts tailored for expert audiences in technical fields would differ markedly from those aimed at laypersons in terms of jargon, detail, and explanation depth. Being audience-aware ensures that AI output meets the practical needs and comprehension levels of its end users.

Conditioning with Feedback Loops

A sophisticated aspect of prompt engineering involves conditioning AI systems through feedback loops.

Engaging in a structured conversation where the system's outputs are iteratively reviewed and redirected based on feedback can fine-tune both the AI understanding and output. This conditioning is particularly effective in sessions where multi-turn interactions are feasible, enabling real-time adaptation and improvement of responses.

Ethical Considerations

Finally, prompt engineering should integrate ethical considerations into its practices. This includes crafting prompts that do not inadvertently encourage the production of biased, harmful, or misleading content.

Users should be aware of potential biases inherent in AI training datasets and actively work to mitigate these through conscientious prompt design. Addressing ethical dimensions promotes responsibility and trust in AI technologies.

In summary, prompt engineering is fundamentally about effective communication with AI systems.

By adhering to the principles of clarity, contextual framing, iterative refinement, format specification, leveraging exemplars, audience-awareness, and ethical responsibility, practitioners can vastly improve the quality and utility of AI outputs. These principles form the core underpinnings of what it means to talk to AI like a pro, transforming abstract potential into practical application.

Chapter 6: Analyzing AI Responses: Feedback for Fine-Tuning

In the intricate dance of human and machine collaboration, prompt engineering serves as the choreography, dictating the movements that lead artificial intelligence (AI) through complex conversations. While crafting effective prompts is an essential skill, equally critical is the evaluation of AI responses.

Analyzing these outputs provides insights that can refine and enhance future interactions. This chapter delves into the methodologies for assessing AI responses, offering a comprehensive guide to the art of feedback for fine-tuning AI systems.

Understanding the Importance of Feedback

Feedback mechanisms are pivotal in the AI training cycle.

They ensure that AI systems are perpetually learning and adapting, enabling improvements not just in responses to specific prompts, but in the overall capacities of these systems to understand and generate human-like text. Feedback informs developers about the alignment of AI responses with expected outcomes, paving the way for strategic interventions that optimize performance.

Criteria for Analyzing AI Responses

Evaluating AI output involves structured criteria to ensure reliability and usability. The following dimensions are crucial in this assessment:

I've seen this happen before: 1.

Relevance and Accuracy: The primary measure of an AI's response is its relevance to the prompt. Does the output pertain directly to the question or task posed? Further, the response must be factually accurate, particularly in domains where precision is non-negotiable, such as medical advice or legal information.

2. **Coherence and Clarity:** Coherence assesses whether the response forms a logical whole, with sentences and ideas connecting seamlessly.

Clarity examines the ease with which a response can be understood. Even an accurate answer loses its value if obscured by convoluted language or poor structure.

3.

Creativity and Originality: For prompts that solicit innovative solutions or creative content, evaluating the originality and inventiveness of the AI's output is key. This involves assessing whether the AI offers novel contributions or merely reiterates well-trodden ideas.

To be honest, 4.

Emotional Intelligence: Particularly in customer service or therapeutic applications, gauging the AI's ability to recognize and appropriately respond to emotional cues can significantly impact user experience. This includes proper tone, empathy demonstration, and supportive language.

5.

Ethical Considerations: Responses must be scrutinized for biases, offensive language, or inappropriate content. Ensuring ethical standards are met is vital in maintaining trust and credibility.

6.

Conciseness and Efficiency: While thoroughness is important, brevity should not be sacrificed. Responses should provide necessary information without unnecessary verbosity, maintaining user's engagement and maximizing efficiency.

Methodologies for Feedback Collection

To refine AI systems through feedback, systematic methodologies must be employed:

1.

Quantitative Scoring Systems: Implement scoring systems where human evaluators rate AI responses on a scale. This structured approach allows for quantitative analysis of performance across various dimensions and enables tracking of improvements over time.

In real life, 2.

Qualitative Annotations: Incorporating detailed qualitative feedback helps identify specific areas of concern or potential. Annotations can indicate where an answer deviated from user expectations or suggest alternative phrasing.

3.

User Feedback and Interaction Logs: Engaging end-users in feedback collection who interact with the AI in real-world settings offers invaluable data. Coupled with interaction logs, this data can unveil recurring issues or patterns in user dissatisfaction or confusion.

4.

A/B Testing: Controlled experiments where different versions of AI are tested against user interactions can highlight which formulation of prompts or responses is more effective. These insights can directly inform prompt engineering strategies.

Processes for Fine-Tuning AI Systems

Feedback serves as the catalyst for continuous improvement, but the actions taken based on this data are where true refinement occurs.

Here's how insights gained from analyses can mold performance enhancement:.

1.

Model Retraining: Incorporate feedback data to retrain AI models. This could mean adjusting parameters, expanding datasets, or even integrating new algorithms that address identified weaknesses in response generation.

It's worth noting that 2.

Prompt Refinement: Use insights about response failures to refine prompt strategies. Adjusting prompts for clarity, specificity, or context can guide AI towards the desired outputs with greater efficacy.

3.

Algorithmic Modifications: For consistent issues traced back to the core functioning of AI, more substantial algorithmic tweaks may be necessary. Developing bespoke solutions that target weak spots allows for leaps in capability over incremental improvements.

4.

Feedback Loop Creation: Establish a robust feedback loop that ensures ongoing assessment and adaptation. Automated processes that flag and resolve repetitive issues can streamline this continuous improvement cycle.

Challenges in Feedback Utilization

While feedback is paramount, several challenges persist in its utilization:

- **Subjectivity in Evaluation:** Human evaluators carry inherent biases, influencing feedback consistency and reliability. Diversifying feedback sources and using metrics to mitigate bias is essential.

It's worth noting that - **Data Overload:** The vast amount of feedback can be daunting to process.

Leveraging AI-driven analytics can distill this wealth of information into actionable insights.

- **Balancing Specificity with Generalization:** While addressing specific feedback is necessary, care must be taken not to overfit models to outliers at the expense of general performance.

Future Directions

Many people don't realize this, but The evolution of AI capabilities hinges on the sophistication of feedback mechanisms.

Future studies may focus on refining these feedback systems using advanced machine learning techniques, exploring adaptive learning algorithms that require minimal human intervention. Moreover, integrating cross-disciplinary insights from cognitive psychology and human-computer interaction could yield breakthroughs in creating more nuanced and proficient AI responses.

Key Takeaway

As AI systems continue to permeate human activities, fine-tuning them through meticulous feedback becomes more pertinent.

By harnessing structured methodologies for feedback collection and leveraging these insights for iterative improvements, we sharpen our prompts, refine AI understanding, and enhance the seamless integration of AI into daily life. In this symbiotic relationship, feedback becomes not merely a reactive tool but a proactive agent of transformative potential.

Chapter 7: Cognitive Psychology and AI Interaction

In the ever-evolving landscape of artificial intelligence, understanding the nuances of human cognition is pivotal to enhancing human-AI interaction.

Cognitive psychology, the scientific study of mental processes such as perception, memory, reasoning, and decision-making, offers invaluable insights into how we can refine our dialogues with AI systems. By leveraging the principles of cognitive psychology, we not only improve our interactions with AI but also maximize the efficiency and effectiveness of these engagements.

The Role of Cognitive Psychology in AI

Let's not forget, Cognitive psychology provides a framework for understanding how humans process information and make decisions.

When it comes to interacting with AI, these foundational insights help inform the design of more intuitive and user-friendly AI systems. At the core, cognitive psychology can guide the development of AI systems that are better attuned to human expectations and behavior patterns.

One of the primary concepts within cognitive psychology is schema theory. Schemas are cognitive structures that help individuals organize and interpret information based on past experiences.

In an AI context, this means designing systems that can predict and accommodate users' anticipated needs and responses. For instance, an AI that understands a user's schema around email communication could automatically prioritize messages based on inferred importance, thereby streamlining user interaction.

Perception and Attention in AI User Interfaces

As strange as it sounds, Perception and attention are critical components of human cognition that impact how users interact with AI systems.

Human perception is selective; it is governed by attention mechanisms that filter out irrelevant information, allowing focus on what is deemed important. This concept is mirrored in AI interfaces through the use of well-designed visual layouts and notification systems that draw the user's attention to critical functionalities or information.

For effective AI interaction, designers must ensure that AI interfaces align with human attentional capacities.

This includes minimizing cognitive overload by reducing unnecessary complexity and emphasizing clarity. For example, an AI-driven dashboard in a financial application should display the most relevant and urgently required information using visual hierarchies, such as larger fonts or contrasting colors, to guide user attention deliberately.

Memory and Learning in AI Interaction

Believe it or not, Memory, another pillar of cognitive psychology, plays a significant role in shaping how users interact with AI systems.

Human memory encompasses short-term memory, where information is temporarily held, and long-term memory, where experiences and knowledge are stored permanently. An AI capable of interacting efficiently with users should take these memory processes into account.

For instance, an AI system may employ techniques such as spaced repetition to reinforce long-term memory retention in educational applications.

By adjusting the intervals between reviews of previously learned material, AI can help maximize learning efficiency and knowledge retention. Moreover, personalization features within AI systems can leverage user data to tailor learning experiences based on previous interactions, effectively building on the user's long-term memory schema.

Reasoning and Decision-Making in AI Systems

Interestingly enough, Human reasoning and decision-making are often influenced by cognitive biases, heuristics, and the framing of information.

Cognitive psychology explores these mechanisms to understand why humans make the choices they do. AI systems can be designed to either complement or counterbalance these human inclinations, thereby optimizing decision-making processes.

For example, within a decision-support AI system, insights from cognitive psychology can inform the presentation of information in a manner that mitigates known biases.

By using techniques such as choice architecture, AI can present users with options in a way that aligns with their values and goals while also safeguarding against impulsive or biased decisions. This is particularly relevant in contexts such as healthcare, where AI might guide practitioners through complex diagnostic processes.

Human-AI Collaboration and Social Cognition

It's worth noting that Social cognition, a subfield of cognitive psychology, delves into how people process, store, and apply information about others and social situations.

Understanding social cognition is essential for designing AI systems that can engage in natural, empathetic interactions with users. By mimicking elements of human social interaction, AI can foster more meaningful and productive collaborations with users.

One practical application of social cognition in AI is the development of natural language processing (NLP) technologies that recognize and appropriately respond to social cues and emotional tones.

An AI chatbot, for instance, should be designed to interpret user sentiment and adjust its responses accordingly—showing empathy in customer service scenarios or delivering encouragement in educational settings.

Implications for AI Design and Development

It's worth noting that When incorporated into AI design and development, the principles of cognitive psychology can significantly enhance user engagement, facilitate learning, improve decision-support systems, and ensure more intuitive user experiences.

Designers and engineers should prioritize a human-centered approach, integrating cognitive psychology insights into the entire lifecycle of AI development.

A concrete strategy involves multidisciplinary collaboration between AI developers, cognitive psychologists, and user experience designers.

By engaging with the expertise from various disciplines, teams can develop AI systems that not only emulate human-like understanding but also anticipate and adapt to users' cognitive processes.

Concluding Thoughts

In real life, The integration of cognitive psychology into AI interaction is not merely a theoretical endeavor; it has profound practical implications for the future of technology.

By fostering a deeper understanding of human cognition, we can create AI systems that are not just tools but partners in an increasingly digital world. As we continue to explore the intersection of AI and cognitive psychology, the potential for innovation in human-computer interaction will only continue to grow, guiding us toward more personalized, efficient, and human-friendly technologies.

Chapter 8: Crafting Precise and Effective Prompts

In the realm of Artificial Intelligence, particularly in the interactions with Language Models, the act of crafting precise and effective prompts stands as a cornerstone skill for realizing the potential of these computational juggernauts.

As AI continues to permeate various aspects of our lives, the task of effectively communicating with it demands not only an understanding of linguistics but also an appreciation for the underlying tech.

Understanding the Core: What is a Prompt?

I've seen this happen before: To understand prompt crafting, one must first dissect the essence of what a prompt is. In its simplest form, a prompt is a set of instructions or inputs that guide an AI model to generate a desired response.

The sophistication of modern Language Models, such as GPT, transcends basic input-output operations, challenging users to harness the intricacies of natural language to elicit precise responses. Think of a prompt as both a question and a key, unlocking a multitude of possibilities stored within the deep learning model.

Crucially, prompts feed onto a tabula rasa of computation, where the sophistication of your input largely determines the depth and relevance of the AI's output.

The objective is to strike a balance where the input is neither overly verbose nor too ambiguous, providing clarity and direction to the model.

Articulating Clarity and Context

To be honest, The bedrock of a powerful prompt is clarity.

A well-articulated prompt is free of ambiguity, enabling the AI to parse the request without misinterpretation. Consider the challenge of guiding a non-sentient linguist through complex navigation; the prompt's role parallels that of a navigator's precise instructions.

1. Avoiding Vagueness: A vague prompt introduces uncertainty and often garners generalized or irrelevant responses.

By leveraging specificity, you delineate the contours of expected output. For example, asking "Tell me about Paris" could yield information ranging from its history to tourist attractions, whereas "Give a brief history of Paris in the 18th century" provides the model with clear coordinates.

2. Establishing Context: Contextual information anchors the model's response within a defined framework.

It is akin to furnishing a backstory that sets the stage for a request. Context may include time frames, subject domains, or the desired form of output such as lists or detailed explanations. By embedding context, you mitigate the potential for tangential discourse.

Structuring Effective Prompts

The architecture of a prompt is a tapestry woven with intent and scope.

Several elements, when combined with strategic foresight, elevate the quality of interaction with AI.

1. Goal Definition: Begin by articulating the end goal of your request.

A clear goal transforms your prompt from a raw query into a purposeful engagement. Manifesting clarity involves pronouncements such as "Summarize," "Compare," or "List," which endow the AI with explicit instructions.

At first glance, **2. Incremental Complexity**: Layered inputs can manage the model's interpretative load, particularly for complex queries.

By parsing a question into bullet points or ordinal lists, you guide the AI step-by-step toward the composite answer. This scaffolded approach mimics the cognitive process of breaking down intricate problems into digestible units.

3. Language Calibration: Tailor the language and vocabulary used within the prompt to align with the expected sophistication of the output.

Technical, academic, or colloquial tones can be elicited based on the choice of diction. For instance, the jargon-laden language of a medical paper leads the AI towards a formal, informative tone.

Experimentation and Feedback

Believe it or not, Though precision in prompt crafting is a learned skill, it thrives in an ecosystem of experimentation and feedback loops.

Given the stochastic nature of AI, a trial-and-error approach is invaluable.

1. Iterative Refinement: A part of the scientific endeavor is refining hypotheses, and prompts are no exception.

Reviewing a series of outputs helps identify lexical or structural adjustments that could enhance future iterations. A sequence of prompt variants, each slightly more refined, can hone your technique.

2. Analysing Outputs: Dissecting the AI's responses offers insights into how prompts are being interpreted.

A pivotal aspect is discerning prevalent bias or errors in the output, which signal areas for prompt improvement. Therefore, critical evaluation stands as both a diagnostic and a learning tool.

The Evolving Nature of Prompts

The art of prompt crafting is not static but evolves in tandem with advancements in AI capabilities and model updates.

This dynamism requires practitioners to stay informed of new features or capabilities within existing models.

**1.

Adapting to Model Updates**: New iterations of language models often come with expanded understandings and capabilities. Adapting to these changes involves keen attention to the underlying nuances in the responding patterns of the AI.

**2.

Community Engagement**: Finally, engaging with peer communities can serve as a lighthouse for navigating uncharted territories in prompt crafting. Collaborative efforts can amplify learning, reveal novel techniques, and foster innovation.

By channeling linguistic prowess through a framework of structured, context-rich prompts, one capitalizes on the full potential of AI models.

In this pursuit, skillful prompt engineering not only enhances communication with AI but uplifts the interaction into a symbiosis of human ingenuity and machine intelligence.

Thus, whether you're an AI enthusiast, a developer, or a scientist, mastering the art of crafting precise and effective prompts is a quintessential tool in your AI toolkit, paving the way for advanced, meaningful engagements with language models at their cutting edge.

Chapter 9: Advanced Techniques for Complex Scenarios

In the rapidly evolving realm of artificial intelligence, particularly in the domain of natural language processing (NLP), the subtlety and efficacy of communication have become paramount.

As AI technologies such as large language models (LLMs) become integral in various industries, understanding advanced techniques in prompt engineering is crucial for optimizing interactions, especially in complex scenarios. This chapter delves into methods for refining prompts to handle intricate tasks, thereby enabling users to leverage AI capabilities to their fullest potential.

Understanding Complexity in AI Tasks

I've seen this happen before: Complex scenarios often require intricate analysis, multi-step reasoning, or a synthesis of diverse data inputs.

These tasks can range from multi-faceted decision-making processes and nuanced sentiment analysis to regulatory compliance checks and dynamic content generation. Unlike straightforward queries, complex scenarios demand a higher level of precision in prompt design.

Decomposition of Tasks

Breaking down a problem into manageable components is an effective strategy frequently employed in engineering and scientific disciplines.

This technique, known as task decomposition, is equally applicable to prompt engineering. The fundamental principle here is to divide a complex query into smaller, more digestible sub-tasks that the AI can address sequentially or in parallel.

For instance, consider the task of generating a comprehensive market analysis report.

Rather than prompting the AI with a broad query such as, "Provide a market analysis report," it can be more effective to deconstruct this into specific sections: assessing current market trends, evaluating key competitors, analyzing customer behaviors, and predicting future market conditions. By segmenting the task, users can craft focused prompts that yield more precise and actionable responses.

Layered Prompting

Layered prompting, another advanced technique, involves the strategic sequencing of queries, building the complexity gradually. This method mimics a conversation where precision is refined with each exchange.

Initially, a broad query sets the context, followed by more targeted questions that incrementally build upon the information obtained previously. This iterative approach enables the AI to deliver more nuanced and layered insights.

To be honest, For example, someone seeking to draft a comprehensive sustainability report may begin with a general question about global sustainability trends before delving into specific industries or regions.

Through successive layers of questioning, the AI can accumulate contextually relevant data, leading to a synthesized and well-informed output.

Leveraging Contextual Embedding

Contextual embedding is a cutting-edge technique in NLP that enhances the model's understanding of context. Advanced LLMs use this technology to capture the semantic nuances of language within a given context.

For prompt engineers, harnessing this feature involves crafting prompts that provide rich contextual information up front. This ensures the AI's responses are highly relevant and contextualized.

Consider a scenario where the AI is tasked with drafting a legal argument.

Here, setting a comprehensive context—such as specifying the legal domain, jurisdiction, relevant statutes, and case precedents—is vital. By embedding detailed context within the prompt, the AI can focus its analysis and generate responses aligned with the intended legal framework.

Utilizing Conditional Logic

Conditional logic in prompts allows for more sophisticated interactions by enabling conditional statements that guide the AI's responses based on specific criteria.

This technique involves posing questions that depend on the fulfillment of certain conditions, akin to the logic used in programming.

As strange as it sounds, For example, when exploring customer feedback on a range of products, a prompt might instruct, "If customer sentiment is negative, analyze common complaints; otherwise, highlight strengths.

" This form of logical structuring enables the AI to adapt its focus dynamically, depending on the contextual data it processes.

Experimentation and Iteration

In complex scenarios, experimentation and iterative refinement of prompts are indispensable. Even seasoned practitioners must engage in trial and error to identify the most effective prompting strategies.

It involves systematically testing variations of prompts and evaluating the nuances of AI responses. This iterative process can illuminate unexpected insights and optimize the prompt's performance.

Furthermore, successful prompt engineering in multifaceted tasks often requires a feedback loop, where the generated outcomes are rigorously assessed and used to refine subsequent prompts.

By applying this scientific method of hypothesis, testing, and refinement, practitioners can significantly enhance the quality and relevance of AI outputs.

Integration with Multimodal Inputs

Advanced LLMs are increasingly capable of processing and synthesizing information from multimodal inputs—such as text, images, and other data types.

In scenarios requiring a holistic analysis, integrating various data modes can yield richer and more diverse insights.

Believe it or not, To illustrate, consider using an AI model to perform an art critique.

A prompt might include links to visual components along with textual descriptions. A cohesive prompt that effectively unifies these modalities will empower the AI to deliver a more comprehensive critique, incorporating visual analysis alongside textual interpretation.

Final Thoughts: Mastery Through Practice

Mastering advanced prompt engineering techniques for complex scenarios is both an art and a science that requires a profound understanding of language models' capabilities coupled with practical experience.

By employing methodologies like task decomposition, layered prompting, contextual embedding, conditional logic, and multimodal integration, practitioners can significantly elevate their interactions with AI. The journey involves continuous learning and refinement, driven by a commitment to optimizing communication with these powerful technologies.

It's worth noting that As AI continues to advance, the landscape of prompt engineering will further evolve, presenting new challenges and opportunities for innovation.

By embracing sophisticated techniques, we can unlock the full potential of AI in complex scenarios, driving progress and efficiency across myriad applications.

Chapter 10: Common Pitfalls and How to Avoid Them

In the burgeoning field of prompt engineering, the interaction between humans and artificial intelligence (AI) is honed to a fine art. While AI models exhibit remarkable capacities, how we communicate with these systems can significantly impact the efficacy, accuracy, and usability of the generated outputs.

Nevertheless, despite tremendous advancements, there are notable pitfalls that users, both novice and experienced, can encounter. Understanding these pitfalls is essential for seamless integration and optimal function of AI applications.

1. Ambiguity in Instructions

Let's not forget, One of the primary pitfalls is the use of ambiguous language in prompts. Ambiguity occurs when a prompt is open to multiple interpretations. The AI, devoid of contextual comprehension, may consequently generate outputs that diverge from the user's original intent.

For example, a prompt like "Describe a bank" could yield information about financial institutions or riverbanks. To sidestep this, specificity should govern prompt construction. Specifying "financial institution" or "riverbank" ensures clarity, guiding the AI toward the desired discourse.

2. Overly Complex Phrasing

In the pursuit of precision, users might default to overly complex language, laden with technical jargon or convoluted sentence structures. While it may seem that complexity equates to better performance, this is often not the case.

AI models thrive on clarity and are optimized for straightforward language. Simplifying phrases while retaining the depth of inquiry enhances understanding and efficiency. Utilizing plain language without sacrificing nuanced detail is key to effective communication with AI systems.

3. Excessive Prompt Length

While striving for detailed prompts, users may inadvertently create prompts that are excessively long. Lengthy prompts can introduce unnecessary complexity and overwhelm the AI, sometimes leading to results that are off-target or diluted in focus.

Optimal prompts are concise yet comprehensive. Establish a balance by distilling content to its essentials, removing superfluous details yet maintaining integral context. This optimization allows the AI to focus sharply on the task at hand.

4. Lack of Contextual Framing

It's worth noting that AI models rely heavily on the context provided within the prompt to generate relevant outputs. A common mistake is the omission of necessary contextual information.

For instance, instructing an AI to "give a summary" without specifying the subject material or document parameters can result in irrelevant or generalized responses. Contextual framing can be enhanced by incorporating precise details such as document titles, authorship, or content themes, thereby enabling the AI to navigate the context more effectively.

5. Neglecting Iterative Feedback

Another frequent pitfall is the failure to engage in iterative refinement practices. Initial interactions with AI may not yield perfect results, requiring users to refine and iterate their prompts based on AI responses.

The iterative feedback loop is crucial for honing outputs to align with the intended outcomes. By continuously calibrating prompts, users can adapt and learn from preliminary results, progressively enhancing the accuracy and relevance of AI-generated content.

6. Overreliance on AI Capabilities

Despite the impressive capabilities of AI, it is vital to recognize its limitations. A pitfall lies in overestimating these systems, expecting them to perform tasks outside their training or understanding.

An example is the assumption that an AI can provide sentiment-driven decisions or interpret nuanced emotional context, a capability that remains limited. To mitigate this, users should align their expectations with the known competencies of the AI and complement AI outputs with human judgment when necessary.

7. Ignoring Ethical Implications

Believe it or not, AI-generated content can influence real-world outcomes, making it imperative to be mindful of ethical considerations.

Common ethical pitfalls include the generation of biased or harmful content, often unintentional, due to deficient prompting or training data biases. Mitigating such pitfalls involves crafting prompts with ethical foresight, scrutinizing AI responses for bias indicators, and employing rigorous review mechanisms before deployment or dissemination.

8. Inadequate Evaluation Criteria

Inadequate setting of evaluation criteria for AI outputs is another frequent pitfall. This can lead to subjective or inconsistent assessment of AI-generated content, complicating the review process and diminishing overall utility.

Users should establish clear, objective benchmarks for evaluating outputs. Utilizing metrics such as relevance, coherence, factual accuracy, and grammatical integrity provides a structured model for assessment, enhancing consistency and reliance on AI-generated materials.

9. Failing to Adapt to Model Updates

AI models are frequently updated, with new versions offering improved accuracy, broader knowledge bases, and refined processing capabilities.

A pitfall arises when users fail to adapt to these updates, continuing to frame prompts based on outdated model parameters. Keeping abreast of changes in AI capabilities and adjusting prompt strategies consequently ensures compatibility and leverages improvements, maximizing the potential benefits from updated models.

10. Overlooking Data Privacy and Security

Many people don't realize this, but Lastly, concerns about data privacy and security constitute critical pitfalls in AI interactions. Prompting AI systems often necessitates the use of sensitive or proprietary information, which, if improperly managed, could result in data breaches or misuse.

Users should adhere to best practices for data privacy, ensure compliance with relevant regulations, and utilize secure channels for input and output exchanges. By prioritizing data security, users protect both organizational interests and individual rights.

In conclusion, the art of prompt engineering is multifaceted, necessitating an informed approach to mitigate common pitfalls.

Awareness and understanding of these pitfalls enable users to craft more effective prompts, refine interactions, and derive maximum utility from AI systems. By implementing these practices, users contribute to the evolution of robust, responsible, and efficient AI communication frameworks, fostering advancements in technology and their applications across various domains.

Chapter 11: Mastering the Art of Contextual Prompts

In the realm of artificial intelligence, especially in the field of natural language processing (NLP), the concept of contextual prompts represents a linchpin for creating effective and coherent interactions between humans and AI systems.

Mastering the art of contextual prompts inevitably demands a deep understanding of not only how language models interpret language but also how they apply context to generate responses. This chapter delves into the intricacies of crafting contextual prompts, offering insights that are both scientifically grounded and practically applicable.

Understanding Contextual Prompts

Contextual prompts are essentially inputs or queries that are designed to provide enough background information for an AI to generate relevant, accurate, and insightful responses.

Unlike standard queries, which might be straightforward questions or commands, contextual prompts harness the power of supplementary information to enrich the interaction.

The role of context in communication, both human and artificial, is paramount. Context determines the meaning and relevance of words and sentences by framing them within a larger narrative or scenario.

For instance, the word "bank" in a sentence about finance typically refers to a financial institution, while in a sentence about rivers, it might mean the land alongside a river. This contextual understanding is crucial for language models to perform accurately.

Structure of Contextual Prompts

I've seen this happen before: Designing effective contextual prompts requires an understanding of both the structure of the prompts and the model's capacity to interpret them.

A well-structured prompt should ideally contain three components: the setup, the goal, and the constraints.

1. **The Setup**: This introduces the main subject or scenario.

It provides background information necessary for the language model to position the response properly. For example, if the task is about developing an itinerary, the setup could include the destination, duration of the visit, and interests of the traveler.

2. **The Goal**: This specifies what you want the AI to achieve.

It should be clear and concise to ensure the AI's response aligns with the user's expectations. Continuing from the previous example, the goal could be to create a budget-friendly itinerary that includes outdoor activities.

Believe it or not, 3.

The Constraints: These define any limitations or specific conditions that the response should adhere to. Constraints might include time limits, budget constraints, or any particular preferences, such as dietary restrictions, in the context of planning.

Techniques for Effective Contextualization

Achieving mastery in creating contextual prompts demands an understanding of techniques that enhance their effectiveness:

At first glance, - **Specify but Don't Overload**: A common pitfall in crafting contextual prompts lies in overwhelming the AI with too much information, leading to confusion or dilution of the core request.

The key is to provide just enough detail to guide the model without inundating it. A precise prompt will typically lead to more relevant responses compared to one that wanders through excessive details.

- **Use of Exemplars**: Providing example scenarios can significantly enhance a model's understanding of context.

This method involves incorporating examples of desired outputs or scenarios within the prompt, thereby guiding the AI through illustrative means.

- **Iterative Refinement**: Crafting effective prompts often requires an iterative approach.

By iterating on prompts and learning from previous outputs, users can progressively hone their queries for improved performance and accuracy. Each iteration is a learning opportunity that informs the next, thus forming an adaptive process.

Real-World Applications

Contextual prompts find their utility in numerous real-world applications, such as customer support chatbots, creative writing aids, and personalized recommendations.

In customer support, for example, contextual prompts can help AI accurately interpret and resolve inquiries by considering the user's interaction history and the context of previous queries.

This personalized approach not only increases the relevance of responses but also enhances user satisfaction and efficiency in issue resolution.

It's worth noting that In creative fields, such as writing or content creation, contextual prompts can assist in generating consistent and style-adherent text by considering the context of previously written material.

This can be particularly beneficial in maintaining narrative coherence in long-form writing tasks.

Challenges in Contextual Prompting

While contextual prompts offer numerous benefits, they are not without challenges. One significant challenge is the inherent ambiguity in human language.

AI systems might struggle with polysemous words and regional expressions, leading to misinterpretations of context. This challenge underlines the necessity of clear and unambiguous prompt design.

Many people don't realize this, but Additionally, there is the issue of balancing depth with breadth.

A prompt that is too narrow may not provide sufficient context, while one that is too broad might overwhelm the AI with possibilities. Finding the optimal balance is an ongoing experiment that involves trial and error.

Chapter Takeaway

In the continuously evolving landscape of artificial intelligence and language processing, the ability to craft effective contextual prompts is an invaluable skill.

By understanding the fundamental components and techniques of contextualization, practitioners can enhance the quality, relevance, and personalization of AI-generated responses. As we refine these techniques through research and practical application, the interactions between humans and machines will become ever more seamless and nuanced, opening doors to innovations yet unseen.

In real life, As we conclude this exploration into contextual prompts, it is imperative to remember that the art of prompting is both a science and a craft.

Like any craft, it requires practice, patience, and a willingness to learn from both successes and setbacks. By embracing these principles, prompt engineers and AI practitioners alike can elevate the quality and effectiveness of human-AI communication to new heights.

Chapter 12: Leveraging AI for Creative Writing and Ideation

In the ever-evolving landscape of artificial intelligence, one domain where AI has increasingly made its mark is in the realm of creative writing and ideation.

This chapter delves into the art and science of harnessing AI tools to assist with generating ideas and producing creative content, providing insights for those looking to enhance their writing process and concept generation capabilities.

At the heart of AI's potential in creative writing lies its ability to process and analyze vast datasets, identifying patterns and generating content that can mimic or augment human creativity.

Natural Language Processing (NLP), a subfield of AI, has seen tremendous advancements, providing the necessary framework for AI to engage with text in meaningful ways. This chapter will explore practical methods to leverage these advances, bridging the gap between human creativity and machine precision.

Understanding AI's Role in Creative Writing

Artificial intelligence can assist writers at multiple stages of the creative process. Through pattern recognition and language generation capabilities, AI systems can produce text that can serve as a foundation or inspiration for human creativity.

However, it is imperative to recognize that AI does not inherently possess creative thought. Instead, it serves as a catalyst that can stimulate and expand the human imagination.

One of the most common implementations of AI in creative writing is through language models such as OpenAI's GPT-3 and its successors.

These models are trained on diverse datasets, enabling them to generate text that can mimic various styles and tones. They can generate poetry, prose, and even scripts, demonstrating an impressive versatility that can be particularly beneficial during the ideation phase.

Developing Initial Ideas

The initial generation of ideas can often be a challenging task for writers.

AI can facilitate this process through prompt-based content creation. By providing the AI with a set of curated prompts or specific parameters, writers can leverage machine-generated content to overcome writer's block and to explore diverse narrative possibilities.

For instance, writers can prompt AI with vague notions such as "a story about an unplanned journey" or more descriptive prompts like "a dialogue between a sentient AI and a skeptical scientist.

" By experimenting with different prompt structures, writers can obtain varied storylines, opening up avenues for creative exploration that might not have been immediately apparent.

Moreover, AI can assist with brainstorming sessions.

When prompted with keywords or themes, AI can quickly generate lists of potential plot points, character ideas, or thematic elements. This versatility allows writers to focus on refining and expanding upon ideas rather than getting bogged down at the conception phase.

Enhancing Drafting and Revising

Once an initial concept is established, AI can be utilized to assist with drafting and revising content.

Language models can generate text based on outlines or fragments provided by the writer, helping to fill in gaps or to propose alternative phrasings. This capacity for dynamic text generation is particularly useful for writers wishing to explore different narrative paths or stylistic approaches.

Believe it or not, When it comes to revising, AI tools equipped with NLP capabilities can be used to suggest edits, improve readability, or ensure consistency in tone and style.

Tools such as Grammarly, Hemingway App, or ProWritingAid are indicative of how AI can enhance the quality of writing by providing real-time feedback on grammar, punctuation, and stylistic concerns.

Moreover, AI can assist in identifying and eliminating biased language or unintentional stereotypes, promoting inclusivity and diversity in writing.

By analyzing text for patterns that may not be overtly apparent to human authors, AI can offer an additional layer of scrutiny, ensuring that creative outputs resonate positively across diverse audiences.

Overcoming Creative Challenges

I've seen this happen before: Creative writing often involves confronting various challenges, from maintaining originality to ensuring coherence across complex narratives.

AI can aid in these areas by functioning as an endless well of inspiration. It can offer novel analogies, unexpected plot twists, or unconventional character arcs, thereby responding to the creative dilemma of originality versus derivativeness.

For instance, when tackling a complex narrative, AI can help track character development and story arcs across different chapters.

By creating a consistent timeline or summarizing past events, AI assists writers in maintaining coherence without resorting to repetitive narrative techniques.

Moreover, when specificity is required, AI can quickly retrieve relevant factual information, ensuring that creative works remain grounded in reality when necessary.

This ability is particularly valuable when incorporating historical contexts, scientific details, or technical terminologies into creative writing.

In real life, #### Critical Considerations and Ethical Implications

While AI offers numerous advantages, it is essential for writers to remain critically engaged with the content AI produces.

Relying too heavily on AI-generated content risks compromising the authenticity and originality that is central to artistry. Writers must view AI as a collaborative tool rather than a crutch, ensuring that their unique voice and perspective remain the driving force behind their creative outputs.

Ethical considerations also warrant attention, particularly concerning ownership and authorship.

As AI-generated content becomes more prevalent, clear guidelines around intellectual property and copyright must be established to protect the rights of human creators. Understanding these ethical landscapes helps authors navigate their collaboration with AI transparently and ethically.

It's worth noting that Ultimately, mastering the art of integrating AI into creative writing involves a delicate balance between utilizing AI's capabilities for enhancement and maintaining the intrinsic elements of human creativity.

By strategically leveraging AI, writers can not only expand their creative potential but also transform the storytelling landscape, crafting narratives that blend the intellect of technology with the depth of human experience.

In conclusion, AI represents a powerful ally in the creative writing process, capable of augmenting the imagination and offering innovative solutions to traditional writing challenges.

As we continue to explore the capabilities of AI, the partnership between human creativity and machine intelligence will undoubtedly yield transformative and enriching possibilities for storytellers and ideators alike.

Chapter 13: AI in Business: Streamlining Communication

In the contemporary business landscape, the role of artificial intelligence (AI) in streamlining communication processes is becoming increasingly pronounced.

As organizations seek to enhance efficiency, reduce costs, and improve customer interaction, AI emerges as a potent tool capable of transforming how businesses communicate internally and externally. This chapter explores the multifaceted impact of AI on business communication, detailing the various technologies involved, their applications, and the practical benefits they offer.

Understanding AI-Powered Communication Tools

Interestingly enough, At the heart of AI-driven business communication are sophisticated algorithms capable of processing and interpreting vast amounts of data at speeds unattainable by humans. These algorithms are employed in an array of tools designed to optimize communication.

Natural Language Processing (NLP) is a cornerstone of these tools, empowering systems to understand and generate human language with a high degree of accuracy. This capability underlies applications ranging from chatbots and virtual assistants to automated email responders and sentiment analysis tools.

Machine learning, a subset of AI, further enhances these systems by enabling them to learn and adapt over time.

Through continuous interaction with users and the assimilation of new data, machine learning algorithms refine their performance, ensuring that communication tools become increasingly intuitive and effective.

Automating Customer Interactions

Interestingly enough, One of the most visible applications of AI in business is the automation of customer service.

Chatbots and virtual assistants are now prevalent across numerous industries, handling a significant portion of customer inquiries. These AI entities can operate 24/7, providing instantaneous responses to common questions and freeing human employees to focus on more complex tasks.

When implemented effectively, AI chatbots elevate customer satisfaction by reducing wait times and providing coherent, prompt responses.

Advanced systems are also capable of emotion detection and personalization. By analyzing a customer's language and tone, these systems can adapt their responses to match users' emotional states, thus fostering a more personalized and empathetic interaction.

For instance, a customer frustrated by delayed shipping can be met with an empathetic response and actionable solutions, thereby enhancing the overall experience, as opposed to receiving a generic reply.

Such tailored interactions are known to increase customer loyalty and improve the brand's reputation.

Enhancing Internal Communication

Beyond customer interactions, AI technologies also play a pivotal role in refining internal communication within businesses.

Tools like AI-powered transcription services can automate meeting summaries, ensuring that all participants have access to comprehensive notes without the need for manual minute-taking. This feature is particularly useful in fast-paced environments where time is of the essence.

Additionally, AI-driven sentiment analysis tools can monitor employee communications to gauge workplace morale and identify potential issues.

By analyzing patterns in emails and chat platforms, organizations can obtain valuable insights into team dynamics and address emerging conflicts proactively.

Let's not forget, Furthermore, AI systems equipped with NLP can facilitate cross-departmental collaboration by translating technical jargon into accessible language, enabling employees from different functions to comprehend complex information effortlessly.

This capability mitigates misunderstandings and improves the efficiency of cross-functional projects.

AI-Driven Decision-Making

In the realm of strategic communication, AI enhances decision-making processes by providing data-driven insights.

AI algorithms capable of analyzing market trends, customer feedback, and competitor activities can inform communication strategies, ensuring they are aligned with the current business environment. By leveraging AI to interpret large datasets, companies can identify potential opportunities and threats, adjust messaging accordingly, and maintain a competitive edge.

At first glance, Moreover, predictive analytics enable businesses to anticipate customer needs and tailor their communication strategies proactively.

By analyzing historical data and customer behavior patterns, AI systems can forecast future trends, guiding the development of marketing and communication campaigns that resonate with target audiences.

Unifying Communication Channels

With the proliferation of communication platforms, businesses face the challenge of ensuring consistency across multiple channels.

AI offers a solution by integrating disparate systems into a cohesive communication ecosystem. Through centralized AI platforms, businesses can manage social media, email, and customer service interactions simultaneously, ensuring a consistent brand voice across all channels.

In real life, AI also enables real-time monitoring of these platforms, allowing businesses to respond promptly to customer inquiries and feedback, thus enhancing the overall customer experience.

By streamlining communication management, AI reduces the risk of misalignment and facilitates a unified, coherent communication strategy.

Challenges and Considerations

Despite the numerous advantages of AI in business communication, there are challenges and considerations that organizations must address.

Data privacy and security remain paramount, as AI systems often require access to sensitive information to function effectively. Businesses must implement robust security measures to protect customer and employee data from breaches and misuse.

In real life, Furthermore, the potential for algorithmic bias poses a significant risk.

AI systems are only as unbiased as the data on which they are trained; thus, businesses must ensure their datasets are diverse and representative to prevent discriminatory outcomes in automated communication processes.

Finally, while AI can significantly enhance communication efficiency, it cannot entirely replace the nuanced understanding and empathy inherent in human interaction.

Businesses must balance the convenience of automation with the necessity of human touch, particularly in sensitive or complex situations where empathy and creativity are crucial.

Key Takeaway

As businesses continue to navigate an increasingly digital landscape, the role of AI in streamlining communication is set to expand.

By automating routine tasks, enhancing customer and internal interactions, informing strategic decisions, and unifying disparate channels, AI offers a myriad of benefits that can significantly improve business communication.

However, the successful integration of AI requires careful consideration of ethical, privacy, and security issues, as well as a balanced approach that recognizes the unique value human communication brings.

As businesses strive to talk to AI like pros, mastering the art and science of prompt engineering is essential to unlocking the full potential of AI-powered communication tools. By doing so, organizations can enhance their operations and build stronger relationships with customers and employees alike, ensuring sustained success in the digital age.

Chapter 14: Ethical Considerations in Prompt Engineering

In the expanding frontier of artificial intelligence, the ability to communicate effectively with AI through prompt engineering is as much an art as it is a science. As AI systems become integral in diverse sectors such as healthcare, finance, education, and entertainment, prompt engineering emerges as a critical tool that shapes AI behavior and decision-making.

However, with great power comes great responsibility. This chapter delves into the ethical considerations inherent in prompt engineering, providing a comprehensive guide for practitioners to engage with AI ethically and responsibly.

The ethical landscape of prompt engineering is multifaceted, encompassing issues of bias, accountability, privacy, transparency, and the potential for misuse.

Understanding these dimensions is crucial for engineers, designers, researchers, and policy makers who aim to harness the benefits of AI while mitigating its risks.

Addressing Bias and Fairness

At the forefront of ethical concerns in prompt engineering is the issue of bias. AI systems trained on historical data can inadvertently perpetuate existing prejudices, leading to biased outcomes.

Prompts, as the guiding inputs for AI, can either exacerbate or alleviate these biases. For instance, a prompt that includes stereotypes or discriminatory language can lead the AI to generate partial or unfair results. To combat this, prompt engineers must critically assess the language they use and strive to create prompts that are neutral, inclusive, and calibrated to diverse perspectives.

Consider a scenario where an AI system assists in hiring decisions.

A prompt that subtly prioritizes certain demographics based on historical hiring data can lead to discriminatory outcomes. Ethical prompt engineering requires engineers to evaluate historical biases within datasets and consciously design prompts that encourage equitable assessments of all candidates, thereby fostering diversity and inclusion.

Ensuring Accountability

With AI systems assuming roles traditionally held by humans, establishing accountability within prompt engineering becomes imperative.

Engineers need to ensure that AI outputs can be traced back to specific prompts and understood within the context they were provided. This traceability is vital for identifying errors and addressing any adverse consequences of AI actions.

For instance, when an AI system provides medical recommendations, engineers must ensure prompts and subsequent outputs are recorded and auditable.

This level of accountability is necessary to verify the validity of the AI's advice and to safeguard patient outcomes. Clearly documenting interactions between prompts and AI outputs creates an ecosystem where responsibilities can be assigned and ethical breaches can be rectified.

Commitment to Privacy

Privacy is another critical dimension of ethical prompt engineering.

As AI systems often require access to sensitive information, engineers must design prompts that respect user privacy and comply with legal frameworks like the General Data Protection Regulation (GDPR). Prompts must be crafted to minimize data exposure, requesting only essential information and ensuring that user data is handled securely.

For example, in personal finance applications where users engage with AI-driven investment advisors, prompts should aim to collect general financial goals and constraints without compromising specific personal data.

Engineers must also implement protocols that allow users to access, modify, or delete their data, thereby reinforcing user control over personal information.

Fostering Transparency and Explainability

Transparency and explainability are cornerstones of ethical AI interactions.

Users need to understand how an AI system arrives at decisions, and prompts play a vital role in facilitating this clarity. Ethical prompt engineering involves crafting prompts that elicit responses in a way that the AI's decision-making process can be easily interpreted by users.

For instance, in legal decision support systems, prompts should guide AI to provide comprehensive reasoning for its recommendations, including the underlying assumptions and evidence considered.

This transparency not only boosts user trust but also enables users to make informed decisions based on AI insights.

Preventing Misuse and Developing Safeguards

The potential for AI misuse is an ever-present concern in prompt engineering.

Malicious actors could design prompts to exploit AI capabilities for unethical purposes, such as generating deepfakes or engaging in social engineering attacks. Engineers must anticipate these possibilities and embed safeguards within the system design to detect and mitigate misuse.

Embedding content filters and employing anomaly detection techniques can help identify and block harmful prompts at an early stage.

Moreover, establishing an ethical framework and a set of best practices for prompt creation can serve as a first line of defense against misuse.

Continuous Ethical Evaluation

Ethical prompt engineering is not a one-time checklist but a continuous process that adapts to evolving societal norms and technological advancements.

Regularly reevaluating the ethical tenets guiding prompt engineering practices is imperative to remain aligned with the best interests of users and society as a whole.

Collaboration between technical experts, ethicists, policymakers, and diverse stakeholder groups can foster a dynamic and responsive ethical framework that proactively addresses emerging challenges.

By staying vigilant and committed to ethical principles, prompt engineers can ensure that AI serves as a force for good, enhancing human capabilities and enriching societal well-being.

As strange as it sounds, In conclusion, the ethical considerations in prompt engineering underscore the dual objectives of harnessing AI's transformative power while safeguarding against its potential risks.

By addressing bias, ensuring accountability, protecting privacy, fostering transparency, preventing misuse, and engaging in ongoing ethical evaluation, prompt engineers can help create an AI landscape that is equitable, trustworthy, and socially responsible. As stewards of AI interactions, prompt engineers bear the vital responsibility of guiding these technologies to serve the greater good, thereby fulfilling the promise of artificial intelligence as an empowering and ethical tool for humanity.

Chapter 15: AI as an Educational Tool: Opportunities and Challenges

In recent years, artificial intelligence (AI) has emerged as a transformative force in education, presenting both unprecedented opportunities and complex challenges. Through its ability to process vast amounts of data and adapt to individual learning patterns, AI has the potential to revolutionize traditional educational paradigms and foster personalized learning environments.

However, alongside these opportunities come significant challenges related to accessibility, ethics, and implementation. This chapter explores the prospects and obstacles associated with the integration of AI in education, offering insights into how educators and institutions can harness its full potential.

Opportunities in AI-Driven Education

1. Personalized Learning:

AI excels in its capacity to tailor educational content to the unique needs of each student.

By analyzing detailed data on student performance, engagement levels, and learning preferences, AI systems can adapt and modify learning materials in real-time. This personalization allows students to progress at their own pace, ensuring that advanced learners are constantly challenged while those needing additional support receive timely interventions.

An AI-driven personalized learning environment can significantly enhance student motivation and retention rates.

Adaptive learning platforms, such as Carnegie Learning's AI-driven tutoring systems, provide examples of how personalized education can complement traditional classroom settings. As AI continues to evolve, it holds the promise of creating bespoke educational experiences that cater to diverse learning styles and abilities.

2. Enhanced Accessibility:

AI has the potential to democratize education by making it more accessible to students with disabilities.

Assistive technologies, powered by AI, can transcribe lectures, convert text to speech, and offer translation services. Speech recognition and natural language processing can help break down barriers for students with visual or auditory impairments.

Furthermore, AI can reach students in remote or underserved regions through online platforms.

Tapping into global educational resources, AI can bridge geographical gaps, allowing students in isolated communities access to the same content as their urban counterparts. OpenAI's use of machine learning to translate difficult texts into simpler language is exemplary of such initiatives.

3. Predictive Analytics:

Predictive analytics, a critical application of AI in education, allows educators to forecast student outcomes and identify at-risk students early.

By analyzing historical data and detecting patterns, AI can provide actionable insights into student performance, allowing educators to implement proactive strategies.

For instance, AI can predict which students are likely to drop out of a course based on engagement metrics, attendance, and performance in assessments.

By providing early warnings, educational institutions can intervene with tailored support services, helping to reduce dropout rates and improve student success.

Challenges in AI Integration

1. Data Privacy and Ethics:

The integration of AI in education raises significant concerns surrounding data privacy and ethics.

AI systems rely on vast amounts of personal data to function effectively, including sensitive information about students' academic performance and personal circumstances. Ensuring robust data protection measures and establishing clear ethical guidelines are paramount to maintaining trust and safeguarding students' privacy rights.

Believe it or not, Moreover, the potential for algorithmic bias poses ethical dilemmas.

AI systems trained on biased datasets may inadvertently propagate existing inequalities, disproportionately affecting marginalized groups. It is essential for educational AI developers to implement rigorous bias detection and mitigation strategies to ensure fairness and equity in education.

2. Teacher Roles and Professional Development:

The rise of AI in education prompts a reevaluation of the traditional role of educators.

While AI can automate administrative tasks and provide supplementary teaching resources, it cannot replace the nuanced and relational aspects of teaching. Educators must adapt to new roles as facilitators of AI-enhanced learning experiences, focusing on critical thinking, creativity, and emotional intelligence—attributes that AI cannot replicate.

At first glance, Professional development programs must be updated to equip teachers with the skills needed to effectively integrate AI into their teaching practices.

Such programs should not only cover technical competencies but also emphasize pedagogical approaches that leverage AI's strengths to enhance learning outcomes.

3. Infrastructure and Resource Allocation:

The successful integration of AI in education depends on adequate infrastructure and resource allocation.

Many educational institutions, particularly in low-income regions, lack the necessary technological infrastructure to support AI deployments. Addressing these disparities requires substantial investment in digital infrastructure and equitable access to technological resources.

It's worth noting that Additionally, the cost of developing and maintaining AI systems can be prohibitive for schools with limited budgets.

Collaborative approaches, such as public-private partnerships, can help alleviate financial constraints, ensuring that AI advancements benefit a broad range of educational contexts.

Final Thoughts

The integration of AI in education presents a dynamic landscape filled with opportunities to enhance learning experiences and challenges that demand careful navigation.

By leveraging its potential for personalized learning, enhanced accessibility, and predictive analytics, AI can play a pivotal role in shaping the future of education. However, addressing data privacy concerns, adapting teacher roles, and ensuring equitable access remain critical to realizing AI's promise.

As educational institutions continue to explore the potential of AI, they must prioritize the development of ethical frameworks and equitable implementation strategies.

By doing so, they can create a balanced AI-driven educational ecosystem that empowers all learners, fosters innovation, and prepares students for a rapidly changing world. Through thoughtful integration and collaboration, AI can be a powerful catalyst for educational excellence and advancement.

Chapter 16: Cross-Cultural Communication in AI Interactions

In an era where artificial intelligence (AI) systems serve as intermediaries in global communication, understanding the nuances of cross-cultural interactions facilitated by AI becomes imperative.

This chapter delves into the scientific intricacies of cross-cultural communication as mediated by AI, exploring how these interactions can be optimized for clarity, efficiency, and cultural sensitivity. Our exploration emphasizes the importance of tailoring AI prompts and interpreting AI responses through the lens of cultural awareness.

The Complexity of Cross-Cultural Communication

Interestingly enough, Cross-cultural communication involves the exchange of information between individuals from different cultural backgrounds. Each culture carries its own set of values, customs, communication styles, and linguistic nuances.

These differences can pose challenges even in face-to-face interactions, potentially leading to misunderstandings or misinterpretations. When introduced into AI interactions, these cultural variables can affect both the input given to AI systems and the output generated by them.

AI systems, particularly those based on natural language processing (NLP), rely on vast datasets to generate responses.

However, these datasets often reflect the cultural biases of their predominant inputs. As a result, AI can inadvertently reinforce cultural stereotypes or misunderstandings unless specifically programmed to understand and adapt to cultural contexts.

Cultural Context in AI Training Data

One key concern in AI cross-cultural communication is the representation, or lack thereof, of diverse cultural contexts in training data.

Many AI models are predominantly trained on data from Western cultures, which may lead to an inherent bias. For instance, idiomatic expressions, cultural references, and communication styles that are normal in one culture might be alien or even offensive in another.

To mitigate such biases, it is crucial to incorporate a more culturally diverse set of data in AI training.

This ensures that AI systems understand different cultural contexts and languages more accurately. Moreover, the AI's ability to recognize and adapt to cultural subtleties can be enhanced through multilingual training sets and context-aware algorithms.

Designing Culturally Responsive Prompts

Creating prompts that are culturally responsive requires an understanding of both language and cultural subtleties.

Here are practical guidelines for designing effective prompts in cross-cultural contexts:.

1. **Simplicity and Clarity**: Use straightforward language to avoid misunderstandings.

Complex sentences or idiomatic expressions can lead to confusion. For instance, instead of saying "hit the nail on the head," consider using "accurately identified. ".

2. **Cultural Neutrality**: When possible, use culturally neutral prompts that do not assume specific cultural knowledge. This minimizes the risk of cultural bias in responses.

Interestingly enough, 3.

Specificity and Context: Provide context within the prompt to guide the AI towards culturally appropriate responses. For example, specifying "in the context of Japanese business etiquette" can help an AI system tailor its advice or response.

4.

Feedback Loops: Include mechanisms for feedback, allowing users to correct or refine AI responses that may be culturally inappropriate or inaccurate. This iterative process aids in improving AI's cultural competencies over time.

Interpreting AI Outputs Through a Cultural Lens

Just as important as crafting effective prompts is the ability to interpret AI outputs with cultural insight.

Users must consider how cultural filters—biases and perspectives shaped by one's own culture—might affect their perception of AI-generated content. Here are some strategies for culturally informed interpretation:.

1.

Awareness of Bias: Be vigilant about potential cultural biases inherent in AI responses. Acknowledge the limitations of AI in capturing the nuances of every culture perfectly.

2.

Cultural Sensitivity: Apply a lens of cultural sensitivity when engaging with AI outputs. This involves understanding contextual cues that might be absent in a culturally biased dataset.

3.

Continuous Learning: Encourage ongoing cultural learning among users who interact frequently with AI. A deeper understanding of diverse cultures can enhance users' ability to critically evaluate AI outputs.

The Future of Cross-Cultural AI Communication

Advancements in AI technology hold promise for improving cross-cultural communication.

Emerging technologies such as zero-shot learning and advanced NLP models are being designed to better decode and generate culturally relevant content. However, the conscious integration of diverse cultural datasets and the application of ethical AI principles remain central to these advancements.

As strange as it sounds, Future AI systems could benefit significantly from collaboration with cultural experts and linguists during the development phase.

Such interdisciplinary cooperation can ensure that AI not only processes information accurately but also respects and adapts to cultural diversity.

Chapter Takeaway: Towards Equitable Global Communication

Cross-cultural communication via AI is not just a technological challenge but a cultural imperative.

As AI continues to bridge communication gaps across the globe, it is essential that these interactions promote equity, respect, and understanding among diverse populations. The principles and strategies outlined in this chapter aim to equip AI users and developers with the tools necessary for fostering meaningful and culturally aware communication in our increasingly interconnected world.

Let's not forget, By approaching AI interactions with cultural intelligence, we move toward a future where AI facilitates, rather than hinders, the rich tapestry of global human communication.

Chapter 17: The Future of AI Language Models and Human Synergy

As we stand at the dawn of a new era in artificial intelligence, the relationship between AI language models and humanity is poised to evolve in ways both profound and nuanced.

The rapid advancements in AI capabilities suggest not just a future replete with technological innovation but also one that will redefine the boundaries of human potential. This chapter delves into the prospective developments in AI language models and examines how these developments will intertwine with human competencies to forge a symbiotic partnership.

The Evolution of AI Language Models

Interestingly enough, To envision the future of AI language models, it is essential to first understand their current capabilities and limitations. Present-day models, such as GPT-3 and its successors, are proficient in generating human-like text, answering complex queries, and engaging in intricate conversations.

They derive their power from vast datasets and sophisticated neural network architectures. However, these models are bound by constraints, such as their dependency on existing data, inability to comprehend context like humans, and lack of genuine understanding.

The next frontier in AI language model development involves overcoming these limitations. Researchers are exploring techniques to enhance the contextual awareness of models, enabling them to understand and generate text with greater coherence and relevance.

Additionally, the integration of multimodal data—such as visual inputs—into language models promises to significantly deepen their interpretive and generative capabilities. Such advancements are anticipated to produce AI systems that exhibit a level of understanding and adaptability closer to that of humans.

Human-AI Collaboration: A Synergistic Future

Interestingly enough, As AI language models advance, their role will increasingly shift from mere tools to collaborative partners. This transition will usher in a new paradigm of human-AI synergy, where the strengths of both entities are harnessed to achieve unprecedented outcomes.

One illustrative area of this synergy is the domain of scientific research. AI language models, with their ability to rapidly analyze and synthesize vast quantities of information, can uncover patterns and insights that may elude human researchers. In turn, human intuition and creativity can guide AI towards more meaningful lines of inquiry, creating a feedback loop that accelerates discovery.

In the creative arts, human-AI collaboration holds the promise of transforming traditional processes.

Writers, musicians, and artists can leverage AI to overcome creative blocks, explore novel styles, or generate preliminary content that inspires further refinement. Importantly, these collaborative efforts are not about AI supplanting human creativity but enhancing it, providing creative professionals with new tools to express their unique visions.

The Intelligence Augmentation Revolution

The ultimate potential of AI language models lies not just in their ability to replace certain tasks or enhance efficiency but in their capacity to augment human intelligence.

This concept, known as intelligence augmentation (IA), envisions a future where AI systems actively amplify human cognitive abilities.

Consider the implications for education: AI language models can provide personalized learning experiences that adapt to individual pacing and comprehension levels.

This tailored approach can facilitate deeper understanding and knowledge retention. Moreover, AI can assist educators in creating more engaging and effective teaching materials, further enriching the learning environment.

In the workplace, IA can alleviate cognitive overload by processing and distilling vast amounts of information, enabling professionals to make more informed decisions.

For instance, in fields such as law or medicine, where staying abreast of new developments is paramount, AI can serve as an ever-vigilant assistant, flagging critical updates and synthesizing complex information into actionable insights.

Ethical Considerations and Challenges

The evolving synergy between AI language models and humans, while promising, is not without ethical considerations and challenges. Issues of bias, transparency, and accountability must be addressed to foster a harmonious coexistence.

AI models are only as unbiased as the data on which they are trained; therefore, ensuring the integrity of training datasets is crucial. As AI systems are increasingly deployed in contexts where ethical judgment is required, there is a pressing need for frameworks that guide the ethical use of AI.

Moreover, the deeper integration of AI into daily life raises concerns about privacy and data security.

As AI language models become more sophisticated, they will inevitably handle more sensitive and personal data. Ensuring that robust security measures are in place, alongside transparent data handling policies, will be integral to building trust in these systems.

A Vision for the Future

Looking ahead, the symbiosis between AI language models and humans holds monumental potential.

The path forward requires a balanced approach that emphasizes both technological innovation and thoughtful deliberation on the social and cultural implications. Stakeholders from diverse fields must collaborate to shape a future where AI enhances human potential without compromising ethical standards.

The future depicted in this chapter is one not solely defined by technological prowess but by the conscious and deliberate choices humanity makes in leveraging that technology.

AI language models, if harnessed responsibly, can become an extension of human intellect and creativity, fostering a world where machines and humans work in concert to overcome the challenges of today and to explore the possibilities of tomorrow.

Interestingly enough, In conclusion, the future of AI language models and human synergy is both inspiring and complex.

By understanding the trajectory of AI advancements and embracing the ideology of collaboration over competition, we can look forward to a future where technology is not merely a tool—but a partner in our collective journey towards knowledge, understanding, and innovation.

Chapter 18: Case Studies: Success Stories in Prompt Engineering

The evolution of Artificial Intelligence (AI) has provided industries with intricate tools that promise to revolutionize various facets of operation and engagement. At the core of these transformative tools is the art of prompt engineering, a critical skill that shapes the way we harness the power of AI models, such as OpenAI's GPT series.

This chapter explores several real-world case studies, showcasing successful applications of prompt engineering across diverse sectors. These success stories illustrate the profound impact that expertly crafted prompts can have on the effectiveness and efficiency of AI deployments.

Case Study 1: Revolutionizing Customer Support in the Financial Sector

I've seen this happen before: One noteworthy instance of effective prompt engineering comes from the financial sector, where a leading bank faced challenges with its customer support services.

The bank's existing manual support system resulted in delayed responses and often failed to satisfy customer inquiries accurately.

The bank integrated an AI-driven chatbot, optimized with tailored prompt engineering. By systematically designing and refining prompts, the AI was trained to recognize nuanced financial terminology and context-specific customer concerns.

For instance, instead of a generic prompt like, "How can I help you today?" the engineers crafted complex prompts such as, "Please describe your issue regarding account transactions or recent payment delays. ".

This refined prompting strategy allowed the chatbot to provide precise assistance, significantly reducing the average response time.

More crucially, customer satisfaction scores increased by 25% over six months, directly attributable to a better understanding and handling of customer queries. The key's success lay in iterative testing and adjustment of prompts, focusing on anticipated customer interactions tailored to specific financial areas.

Many people don't realize this, but #### Case Study 2: Enhancing Content Generation for Digital Marketing

In the realm of digital marketing, creating engaging content that captures audience interest is vital.

A global marketing agency sought to enhance its content creation process using an AI writing assistant. Initial attempts resulted in content that, although grammatically correct, lacked authentic engagement and alignment with brand voice, crucial for maintaining audience connection.

The breakthrough came with innovative prompt engineering, where marketers collaborated with AI specialists to craft prompts that emulated the desired tone and style. They developed detailed instruction sets for the AI, such as, "Generate a social media post introducing a new eco-friendly product.

Use an enthusiastic and relatable tone while emphasizing sustainability. ".

Interestingly enough, Through prompt refinement, the AI achieved greater alignment with the brand's voice and significantly improved engagement metrics.

Website traffic and user interaction rates surged following the introduction of AI-generated content. Additionally, the agency reduced its content production cycle by 40%, allowing for more frequent updates and greater audience engagement.

Case Study 3: Streamlining Educational Technology

Educational institutions consistently explore innovative methods to bolster learning experiences.

At a university specializing in STEM, educators sought an AI solution to provide personalized tutoring for introductory computer science students.

It's worth noting that By employing advanced prompt engineering techniques, educators created a virtual tutor that adaptively responded to the student's comprehension level. Instead of static question-and-answer prompts, the system used prompts like, "Explain how a loop works in Python.

Include examples and analogies comparing it to everyday tasks that resonate with beginners. ".

Such prompts enabled the AI to deliver custom-tailored explanations, supporting diverse learning paces and styles.

The application of refined prompts led to a measurable improvement in student performance, with course pass rates increasing by 15%. Furthermore, the virtual tutor equipped students with a deeper understanding of programming fundamentals, fostering robust learning outcomes.

Common Threads in Success

I've seen this happen before: The case studies presented accentuate how careful and intentional prompt engineering can vastly alter the impact AI can have in practice.

Across each example, several common threads emerge:.

1.

Context Awareness: Designing prompts that incorporate specific knowledge relevant to the domain fosters more accurate and useful AI responses. Domain-specific lexicon and customer needs are carefully considered.

2. **Iterative Development**: All success stories emphasized a feedback-driven, iterative process that allowed for continuous refinement of prompts for optimal results.

Believe it or not, 3.

Multidisciplinary Collaboration: Effective prompt engineering often requires a team that combines AI expertise with industry-specific knowledge, enabling comprehensive understanding and nuanced application.

4. **End-User Focus**: Prioritizing the end-user experience, whether it's a consumer, student, or client, ensures that the AI provides high-value and relevant engagement.

The integration of AI through strategic prompt engineering exemplifies not just technological advancement but the critical application of human insight and creativity.

As we deepen our capabilities with AI, the art and science of prompt engineering will continue to shape groundbreaking pathways toward innovation and efficiency across industries.

Chapter 19: Prompt Engineering Tools and Technologies

In the rapidly evolving landscape of artificial intelligence, particularly within the realm of natural language processing (NLP) and generation, prompt engineering has emerged as a critical skill.

Effective prompt engineering can significantly enhance the performance and utility of AI models by crafting queries that elicit the most accurate and relevant responses. This chapter delves into the various tools and technologies that facilitate prompt engineering, enabling practitioners to harness the full potential of AI language models.

19.1 The Foundations of Prompt Engineering Tools

At first glance, Prompt engineering tools are specifically designed to interact with AI models, allowing users to experiment with different query structures and parameters to achieve optimal results.

These tools are indispensable for researchers, developers, and practitioners seeking to optimize AI interactions. They typically offer interfaces and features that simplify the process of testing and refining prompts, making them accessible to both novice users and experts.

At the core of these tools is their capability to abstract the complexity of AI model interactions.

They provide user-friendly interfaces, often coupled with powerful back-end processing that communicates directly with state-of-the-art language models. This abstraction allows users to focus on crafting effective prompts without delving into the intricacies of AI architecture.

19.2 Interactive Platforms for Prompt Design

In real life, Among the most popular tools are interactive platforms that allow for the real-time design and testing of prompts.

These platforms generally provide a workspace where users can input queries, immediately see the responses generated by the AI, and iteratively refine their prompts based on the outcomes.

OpenAI Playground is an example of such a platform. It allows users to experiment with its models through a simple interface where one can type a prompt and instantly receive a response.

Users can adjust various settings such as temperature, which influences the randomness and creativity of the generated output, and maximum token count, which determines the length of the response. The interactive nature of these platforms supports a trial-and-error approach, which is crucial for mastering prompt engineering.

19.3 Specialized Programming Libraries and APIs

Interestingly enough, In addition to interactive platforms, programming libraries and APIs offer programmatic access to AI models for more custom and scalable solutions.

Libraries such as **Transformers** by Hugging Face provide extensive tools for deploying and fine-tuning language models. These libraries are indispensable for developers looking to embed AI models within applications, enabling them to programmatically generate, test, and refine prompts.

Hugging Face's Transformers library, for instance, offers pre-trained models and utilities for customizing model parameters.

Through its API, developers can submit prompts and process the outputs in a way that integrates seamlessly with applications, allowing for automated and dynamic prompt generation.

19.4 Visualization Tools for Prompt Analysis

In real life, Understanding AI model responses necessitates not just crafting prompts but also analyzing the outputs.

Visualization tools play a pivotal role in this aspect of prompt engineering. Tools like **TensorBoard** and custom visualization scripts can be used to graphically interpret the performance of different prompts, providing insights into how variations in query structure affect the quality of the AI's responses.

This analytical capability is crucial for refining prompts to optimize their effectiveness.

By visualizing metrics such as relevance scores, coherence, and novelty of responses, practitioners can identify patterns and correlations that inform further prompt refinement.

19.5 Data Annotation and Evaluation Platforms

As strange as it sounds, Data annotation tools are another category of technology integral to prompt engineering.

Platforms such as **Labelbox** and **Scale AI** facilitate the classification and annotation of AI outputs, enabling users to evaluate the efficacy of their prompts systematically. By annotating which AI responses accurately meet the desired criteria, users can create datasets that guide future prompt development.

These annotation tools often integrate with feedback systems, allowing users to rate the quality of outputs and provide corrective inputs.

This feedback loop is essential for continuously improving the AI model's ability to interpret and respond to complex queries.

19.6 Collaborative and Community-driven Tools

In real life, Community-driven platforms offer collaborative environments where prompt engineers can share insights, trial and error experiences, and best practices.

Kaggle, for instance, provides a community where AI enthusiasts and professionals can collaborate on machine learning challenges, often involving elements of prompt engineering.

Through these collaborative environments, practitioners can access shared repositories of prompts, scripts, and experiments.

This exchange of information accelerates the learning process and fosters innovation in prompt engineering techniques.

19.7 The Importance of Security and Ethical Considerations

At first glance, With the power of AI models come significant responsibilities, particularly in ensuring secure and ethical use.

Trusted prompt engineering tools incorporate features that allow users to anonymize data, control access levels, and audit interactions with AI models. Technologies like **differential privacy** and **encrypted data processing** are increasingly integrated into systems to ensure compliance with ethical standards and privacy laws.

Ensuring that prompt engineering activities adhere to ethical guidelines involves more than just tool functionality; it requires an overarching commitment to transparency and accountability.

This includes usage monitoring, transparent logging of queries, and providing users with clear guidelines on ethical AI interactions.

In conclusion, prompt engineering tools and technologies are foundational to effective AI model interaction. They provide the necessary infrastructure for testing, refining, and deploying prompts that elicit robust and meaningful AI responses.

By leveraging these technologies, practitioners can unlock the full potential of language models, driving innovation and delivering intelligent solutions in a myriad of applications. As these tools evolve, they will continue to be an essential component in the toolkit of anyone involved in the art and science of talking to AI like a pro.

Chapter 20: Conclusion: Embracing AI as a Collaborative Partner

In recent years, the dynamic interplay between humans and artificial intelligence (AI) systems has ushered in a new era of possibilities. As we conclude this exploration into prompt engineering, it becomes essential to synthesize our understanding of AI as a collaborative partner.

Throughout this book, we have uncovered not only the nuances of crafting effective prompts but also the broader implications of engaging with AI. This chapter aims to consolidate these insights and highlight the transformative potential of AI-human collaboration.

The Reciprocity of Intelligence

As strange as it sounds, The essence of AI as a collaborative partner lies in its ability to augment human intelligence rather than supplant it. Unlike purely autonomous systems, AI that operates under the guidance of prompt engineering thrives on the reciprocity of intelligence.

This means humans provide strategic direction through well-crafted prompts, while the AI contributes computational power and pattern recognition capabilities. This synergy allows for the co-creation of solutions that transcend the limitations of solitary human or machine endeavor.

Prompt engineering, as discussed throughout this book, is the artful construction of inputs that guide AI towards desired outputs. It requires a deep understanding of both the task at hand and the capabilities of the AI model.

The prompts act as the bridge between human intention and machine execution, translating complex human queries into actionable tasks for the AI. A successful prompt harnesses the AI's potential, crafting precise dialogues that ensure clarity and relevance in the responses generated.

Integrating AI into Decision-Making Processes

Interestingly enough, AI's role as a collaborative partner reaches beyond mere task execution; it becomes integral to decision-making processes across diverse fields.

In healthcare, for example, AI systems assist in diagnosing diseases by analyzing vast datasets of medical imaging and patient history. The deployment of AI in such scenarios illustrates its capability to provide evidence-based insights that guide expert decisions.

Similarly, in business settings, AI assists in trend analysis and forecasting.

By parsing through immense quantities of data, AI systems offer strategic recommendations, guiding organizational leaders in making informed choices. Here again, prompt engineering serves as a crucial interface: only by posing the right questions can AI yield meaningful and applicable insights.

The efficacy of AI as a collaborative partner in decision-making is contingent upon the continuous refinement of both the AI's algorithms and human expertise in prompt engineering.

This interplay ensures that AI remains an asset that complements human judgment rather than a replacement for it.

Ethical Considerations and Trust

As we increasingly integrate AI into our collaborative frameworks, considerations surrounding ethics and trust become paramount.

AI systems, like any tool, can be wielded for purposes that align with human values or diverge from them. Therefore, prompt engineers must approach their craft with a conscientious understanding of these dynamics.

Ensuring transparency in AI operations is a critical element in fostering trust.

Users must have insight into how AI systems process information and generate responses. This transparency builds confidence in the outputs provided by AI, particularly in sensitive areas such as healthcare, finance, and law.

Interestingly enough, Moreover, the ethical design of AI systems involves actively avoiding biases and ensuring fairness in AI-driven decisions.

A meticulous examination of datasets used to train AI models is necessary to prevent perpetuation of historical inequalities or prejudices. Here, prompt engineers must take responsibility not only for the outputs generated by their crafted prompts but also for the biases that may be unintentionally encoded into AI systems.

The Future of Human-AI Collaboration

Envisioning the future of AI as a collaborative partner entails an optimistic view of technological progress.

As AI systems become increasingly adept at understanding and processing human language, the role of prompt engineering will continue to evolve. Future AI models may not only respond to prompts with increased accuracy but also engage in more nuanced and context-aware interactions.

I've seen this happen before: One exciting prospect is the development of AI systems capable of autonomous learning from interactive dialogues.

Such systems could adjust their responses based on user feedback, creating a dynamic learning environment where AI becomes progressively more attuned to individual user preferences and industry-specific language.

Additionally, the democratization of AI tools will open new frontiers for collaboration, empowering professionals from various fields who may not have deep technical expertise in AI.

By lowering the entry barriers to effective prompt engineering, a broader array of users can harness AI's potential, fostering a more inclusive technological landscape.

Concluding Thoughts

I've seen this happen before: Throughout this book, we have delved into the intricacies of prompt engineering, highlighting its pivotal role in human-AI collaboration.

As we stand on the cusp of widespread AI integration across industries, it is imperative to view AI not simply as a tool but as a partner with unique capabilities that enhance human creativity and problem-solving.

Embracing AI as a collaborative partner involves recognizing its strengths and limitations, ensuring ethical considerations, and continually refining our approach to prompt engineering.

As we move forward, the art and science of interacting with AI will demand both technological fluency and a commitment to ethical stewardship. It is through this dual lens that we can fully realize the transformative potential of AI, crafting a future where human ingenuity and artificial intelligence converge in harmonious collaboration.

About the Author

T. S. AVINI is a writer who believes in the power of sharing life's lessons. Having faced hardship and pain, he turned to writing as a form of self-expression and healing. Today, he pours his heart into every book, aiming to help others navigate their own struggles and find strength in vulnerability.